C000090195

1935 if you wanted to
read a good book, you needed
either a lot of money or a library card.
Cheap paperbacks were available, but their
poor production generally mirrored the quality
between the covers. One weekend that year,
Allen Lane, Managing Director of The Bodley Head,
having spent the weekend visiting Agatha Christie,
found himself on a platform at Exeter station trying to
find something to read for his journey back to London.
He was appalled by the quality of the material he had to
choose from. Everything that Allen Lane achieved from that
day until his death in 1970 was based on a passionate belief
in the existence of 'a vast reading public for *intelligent*
books at a low price'. The result of his momentous vision
was the birth not only of Penguin, but of the 'paperback
revolution'. Quality writing became available for the price of
a packet of cigarettes, literature became a mass medium
for the first time, a nation of book-borrowers became a
nation of book-buyers – and the very concept of book
publishing was changed for ever. Those founding
principles – of quality and value, with an overarching
belief in the fundamental importance of reading –
have guided everything the company has
done since 1935. Sir Allen Lane's
pioneering spirit is still very much alive
at Penguin in 2005. Here's to
the next 70 years!

MORE THAN A BUSINESS

'We decided it was time to end the almost customary half-hearted manner in which cheap editions were produced – as though the only people who could possibly want cheap editions must belong to a lower order of intelligence. We, however, believed in the existence in this country of a vast reading public for intelligent books at a low price, and staked everything on it'
Sir Allen Lane, 1902–1970

'The Penguin Books are splendid value for sixpence, so splendid that if other publishers had any sense they would combine against them and suppress them'
George Orwell

'More than a business … a national cultural asset'
Guardian

'When you look at the whole Penguin achievement you know that it constitutes, in action, one of the more democratic successes of our recent social history'
Richard Hoggart

Happy Birthday, Jack Nicholson

HUNTER S. THOMPSON

PENGUIN BOOKS

PENGUIN BOOKS

Published by the Penguin Group
Penguin Books Ltd, 80 Strand, London WC2R 0RL, England
Penguin Group (USA) Inc., 375 Hudson Street, New York, New York 10014, USA
Penguin Group (Canada), 10 Alcorn Avenue, Toronto, Ontario, Canada M4V 3B2
(a division of Pearson Penguin Canada Inc.)
Penguin Ireland, 25 St Stephen's Green, Dublin 2, Ireland
(a division of Penguin Books Ltd)
Penguin Group (Australia), 250 Camberwell Road, Camberwell, Victoria 3124,
Australia (a division of Pearson Australia Group Pty Ltd)
Penguin Books India Pvt Ltd, 11 Community Centre,
Panchsheel Park, New Delhi – 110 017, India
Penguin Group (NZ), cnr Airborne and Rosedale Roads, Albany,
Auckland 1310, New Zealand (a division of Pearson New Zealand Ltd)
Penguin Books (South Africa) (Pty) Ltd, 24 Sturdee Avenue,
Rosebank 2196, South Africa

Penguin Books Ltd, Registered Offices: 80 Strand, London WC2R 0RL, England

www.penguin.com

Kingdom of Fear first published in the USA by Simon & Schuster 2003
First published in Great Britain by Allen Lane 2003
These extracts published as a Pocket Penguin 2005

1

Copyright © Gonzo International Corp., 2003
All rights reserved

The moral right of the author has been asserted

Set in 11/13pt Monotype Dante
Typeset by Palimpsest Book Production Limited
Polmont, Stirlingshire
Printed in England by Clays Ltd, St Ives plc

Contents

The Mailbox: Louisville, Summer of 1946

My parents were decent people, and I was raised, like my friends, to believe that Police were our friends and protectors – the Badge was a symbol of extremely high authority, perhaps the highest of all. Nobody ever asked *why*. It was one of those unnatural questions that are better left alone. If you had to ask *that*, you were sure as hell Guilty of *something* and probably should have been put behind bars a long time ago. It was a no-win situation.

My first face-to-face confrontation with the FBI occurred when I was nine years old. Two grim-looking Agents came to our house and terrified my parents by saying that I was a 'prime suspect' in the case of a Federal Mailbox being turned over in the path of a speeding bus. It was a Federal offense, they said, and carried a five-year prison sentence.

'Oh no!' wailed my mother. 'Not in prison! That's insane! He's only a child. How could he have known?'

'The warning is clearly printed on the Mailbox,' said the agent in the gray suit. 'He's old enough to read.'

'Not necessarily,' my father said sharply. 'How do you know he's not blind, or a moron?'

'Are you a moron, son?' the agent asked me. 'Are you blind? Were you just *pretending* to read that newspaper when we came in?' He pointed to the *Louisville Courier-Journal* on the couch.

'That was only the sports section,' I told him. 'I can't read the other stuff.'

'See?' said my father. 'I told you he was a moron.'

'Ignorance of the law is no excuse,' the brown-suit agent replied. 'Tampering with the US Mail is a Federal offense punishable under Federal law. That Mailbox was badly damaged.'

Mailboxes were huge, back then. They were heavy green vaults that stood like Roman mile markers at corners on the neighborhood bus routes and were rarely, if ever, moved. I was barely tall enough to reach the Mail-drop slot, much less big enough to turn the bastard over and into the path of a bus. It was clearly impossible that I could have committed this crime without help, and that was what they wanted: names and addresses, along with a total confession. They already knew I was guilty, they said, because other culprits had squealed on me. My parents hung their heads, and I saw my mother weeping.

I had done it, of course, and I had done it with plenty of help. It was carefully plotted and planned, a deliberate ambush that we set up and executed with the fiendish skill that smart nine-year-old boys are capable of when they have too much time on their hands and a lust for revenge on a rude and stupid bus driver who got a kick out of closing his doors and pulling away just as we staggered to the top of the hill and begged him to let us climb on . . . He was new on the job, probably a brain-damaged substitute, filling in for our regular driver, who was friendly and kind and always willing to wait a few seconds for children rushing to school. Every kid in the neighborhood agreed that this new swine of a driver was a sadist who deserved to be punished, and the Hawks AC were the ones to do it. We saw it more as a duty than a prank. It was a brazen Insult to the honor of the whole neighborhood.

We would need ropes and pulleys and certainly no witnesses to do the job properly. We had to tilt the iron monster so far over that it was perfectly balanced to fall instantly, just as the fool zoomed into the bus stop at his usual arrogant speed. All that kept the box more or less upright was my grip on a long 'invisible' string that we had carefully stretched all the way from the corner and across about 50 feet of grass lawn to where we crouched out of sight in some bushes.

The rig worked perfectly. The bastard was right on schedule and going too fast to stop when he saw the thing falling in front of him . . . The collision made a horrible noise, like a bomb going off or a freight train exploding in Germany. That is how I remember it, at least. It was the worst noise I'd ever heard. People ran screaming out of their houses like chickens gone crazy with fear. They howled at one another as the driver stumbled out of his bus and collapsed in a heap on the grass . . . The bus was empty of passengers, as usual at the far end of the line. The man was not injured, but he went into a foaming rage when he spotted us fleeing down the hill and into a nearby alley. He knew in a flash who had done it, and so did most of the neighbors.

'Why deny it, Hunter?' said one of the FBI agents. 'We know *exactly* what happened up there on that corner on Saturday. Your buddies already confessed, son. They *squealed* on you. We know you did it, so don't lie to us now and make things worse for yourself. A nice kid like you shouldn't have to go to Federal prison.' He smiled again and winked at my father, who responded with a snarl: 'Tell the Truth, damn it! Don't lie to these men. They have *witnesses!*' The FBI agents nodded grimly at each other and moved as if to take me into custody.

It was a magic moment in my life, a defining instant for me or any other nine-year-old boy growing up in the 1940s after World War II – and I clearly recall thinking: *Well, this is it. These are G-Men . . .*

WHACK! Like a flash of nearby lightning that lights up the sky for three or four terrifying split seconds before you hear the thunder – a matter of *zepto-seconds* in real time – but when you are a nine-year-old boy with two (2) full-grown FBI agents about to seize you and clap you in Federal prison, a few quiet zepto-seconds can seem like the rest of your life . . . And that's how it felt to me that day, and in grim retrospect, I was right. They had me, dead to rights. I was Guilty. Why deny it? Confess Now, and throw myself on their mercy, or –

What? What if I *didn't* confess? That was the question. And I was a curious boy, so I decided, as it were, to roll the dice and ask *them* a question.

'Who?' I said. 'What witnesses?'

It was not a hell of a lot to ask, under those circumstances – and I really did want to know exactly who among my best friends and blood brothers in the

4

dreaded Hawks AC had cracked under pressure and betrayed me to these thugs, these pompous brutes and toadies with badges & plastic cards in their wallets that said they worked for J. Edgar Hoover and that they had the Right, and even the duty, to put me in jail, because they'd heard a 'Rumor in the neighborhood' that some of my boys had gone belly up and rolled on me. *What?* No. Impossible.

Or not *likely*, anyway. Hell, Nobody squealed on the Hawks AC, or not on its President, anyway. Not on Me. So I asked again: 'Witnesses? What Witnesses?'

And that was all it took, as I recall. We observed a moment of silence, as my old friend Edward Bennett Williams would say. Nobody spoke – especially not me – and when my father finally broke the eerie silence, there was *doubt* in his voice. 'I think my son has a point, officer. Just exactly who *have* you talked to? I was about to ask that myself.'

'Not Duke!' I shouted. 'He went to Lexington with his father! And not *Ching*! And not *Jay*! –'

'Shut up,' said my father. 'Be quiet and let *me* handle this, you fool.'

And that's what happened, folks. We never saw those FBI agents again. Never. And I learned a powerful lesson: Never believe the first thing an FBI agent tells you about anything – especially not if he seems to believe you are guilty of a crime. Maybe he has no evidence. Maybe he's bluffing. Maybe you are innocent. Maybe. The Law can be hazy on these things . . . But it is definitely worth a roll.

In any case, nobody was arrested for that alleged incident. The FBI agents went away, the US Mailbox was put back up on its heavy iron legs, and we never saw that drunken swine of a substitute bus driver again.

Strange Lusts and Terrifying Memories

My father had a tendency to hunch darkly over the radio when the news of the day was foul. We listened to the first wave of Pearl Harbor news together. I didn't understand it, but I knew it was bad because I saw him hunch up like a spider for two or three days in a row after it happened. 'God damn those sneaky Japs,' he would mutter from time to time. Then he would drink whiskey and hammer on the arm of the couch. Nobody else in our family wanted to be with him when he listened to the war news. They didn't mind the whiskey, but they came to associate the radio with feelings of anger and fear.

I was not like that. Listening to the radio and sipping whiskey with my father was the high point of my day, and I soon became addicted to those moments. They were never especially happy, but they were always exciting. There was a certain wildness to it, a queer adrenaline rush of guilt and mystery and vaguely secret joy that I still can't explain, but even at the curious age of four I knew it was a special taste that I shared only with my father. We didn't dwell on it, or feel a dark need to confess. Not at all. It was fun, and I still enjoy remembering those hours when we hunched together beside the radio with our whiskey and our war and our fears about evil Japs sneaking up on us . . .

I understand that fear is my friend, but not always. Never turn your back on Fear. It should always be in front of you, like a thing that might have to be killed. My father taught me that, along with a few other things that have kept my life interesting. When I think of him now I think of fast horses and cruel Japs and lying FBI agents.

'There is no such thing as Paranoia,' he told me once. 'Even your Worst fears will come true if you chase them long enough. Beware, son. There is Trouble lurking out there in that darkness, sure as hell. Wild beasts and cruel people, and some of them will pounce on your neck and try to tear your head off, if you're not careful.'

It was a mean piece of wisdom to lay on a 10-year-old boy, but in retrospect I think it was the right thing to say, and it definitely turned out to be true. I have wandered into that darkness many times in my life and for many strange reasons that I still have trouble explaining, and I could tell you a whole butcher shop full of stories about the horrible savage beasts that lurk out there, most of them beyond the wildest imagination of a 10-year-old boy – or even a 20- or 30-year-old boy, for that matter, or even beyond the imagination of a teenage girl from Denver being dragged away from her family by a pack of diseased wolves. Nothing compares to it. The terror of a moment like that rolls over you like a rush of hot scum in a sewer pipe.

Where Were You when the Fun Stopped?

There was no laughter tonight, only the sounds of doom and death and failure – a relentless torrent of death signals: from the sheriff, in the mail, on the phone, in my kitchen, in the air, but mainly from Maria, who said she felt it very strongly and she understood exactly why I was feeling and thinking the way I did/do, but there was nothing she could do about it. She couldn't help herself. It was the death of fun, unreeling right in front of us, unraveling, withering, collapsing, draining away in the darkness like a handful of stolen mercury. Yep, the silver stuff goes suddenly, leaving only a glaze of poison on the skin.

September 11, 2001

It was just after dawn in Woody Creek, Colorado, when the first plane hit the World Trade Center in New York City on Tuesday morning, and as usual I was writing about sports. But not for long. Football suddenly seemed irrelevant compared to the scenes of destruction and utter devastation coming out of New York on TV.

Even ESPN was broadcasting war news. It was the worst disaster in the history of the United States, including Pearl Harbor, the San Francisco earthquake, and the Battle of Antietam in 1862, when 23,000 were slaughtered in one day.

The Battle of the World Trade Center lasted about 99 minutes and cost 20,000 lives in two hours (according to unofficial estimates as of midnight Tuesday). The final numbers, including those from the supposedly impregnable Pentagon, across the Potomac River from Washington, likely will be higher. Anything that kills 300 trained firefighters in two hours is a world-class disaster.

And it was not even Bombs that caused this massive damage. No nuclear missiles were launched from any foreign soil, no enemy bombers flew over New York and Washington to rain death on innocent Americans. No. It was four commercial jetliners.

They were the first flights of the day from American and United Airlines, piloted by skilled and loyal US citizens, and there was nothing suspicious about them when they took off from Newark, NJ, Dulles in DC, and Logan in Boston on routine cross-country flights to the West Coast with fully loaded fuel tanks – which would soon explode on impact and utterly destroy the world-famous Twin Towers of downtown Manhattan's World Trade Center. Boom! Boom! Just like that.

The towers are gone now, reduced to bloody rubble, along with all hopes for Peace in Our Time, in the United States or any other country. Make no mistake about it: We are At War now – with somebody – and we will stay At War with that mysterious Enemy for the rest of our lives.

It will be a Religious War, a sort of Christian Jihad, fueled by religious hatred and led by merciless fanatics on both sides. It will be guerilla warfare on a global scale, with no front lines and no identifiable enemy. Osama bin Laden may be a primitive 'figurehead' – or even dead, for all we know – but whoever put those All-American jet planes loaded with All-American fuel into the Twin Towers and the Pentagon did it with chilling precision and accuracy. The second one was a dead-on bull's-eye. Straight into the middle of the skyscraper.

Nothing – not even George Bush's $350 billion 'Star Wars' missile defense system – could have prevented Tuesday's attack, and it cost next to nothing to pull off. Fewer than 20 unarmed Suicide soldiers from some apparently primitive country somewhere on the other side of the world took out the World Trade Center and half the Pentagon with three quick and costless strikes on one day. The efficiency of it was terrifying.

We are going to punish somebody for this attack, but just who or what will be blown to smithereens for it is hard to say. Maybe Afghanistan, maybe Pakistan or Iraq, or possibly all three at once. Who knows? Not even the Generals in what remains of the Pentagon or the New York papers calling for WAR seem to know who did it or where to look for them.

This is going to be a very expensive war, and Victory is not guaranteed – for anyone, and certainly not for anyone as baffled as George W. Bush. All he knows is that his father started the war a long time ago, and that he, the goofy child-President, has been chosen by Fate and the global Oil industry to finish it Now. He will declare a National Security Emergency and clamp down Hard on Everybody, no matter where they live or why. If the guilty won't hold up their hands and confess, he and the Generals will ferret them out by force.

Good luck. He is in for a profoundly difficult job – armed as he is with no credible Military Intelligence, no witnesses, and only the ghost of bin Laden to blame for the tragedy.

OK. It is 24 hours later now, and we are not getting much information about the Five Ws of this thing.

The numbers out of the Pentagon are baffling, as if Military Censorship has already been imposed on the media. It is ominous. The only news on TV comes from weeping victims and ignorant speculators.

The lid is on. Loose Lips Sink Ships. Don't say anything that might give aid to The Enemy.

September 12, 2001

Johnny Depp called me from France on Sunday night and asked what I knew about Osama bin Laden.

'Nothing,' I said. 'Nothing at all. He is a ghost, for all I know. Why do you ask?'

'Because I'm terrified of him,' he said. 'All of France is terrified . . . I freaked out and rushed to the airport, but when I got there my flight was canceled. All flights to the US were canceled. People went crazy with fear.'

'Join the club,' I told him. 'Almost everybody went crazy over here.'

'Never mind that,' he said. 'Who won the Jets–Colts game?'

'There *was* no game,' I said. 'All sports were canceled in this country – even *Monday Night Football*.'

'No!' he said. 'That's impossible! I've never known a Monday night without a game on TV. What is the stock market doing?'

'Nothing yet,' I said. 'It's been closed for six days.'

'Ye gods,' he muttered. 'No stock market, no football – this is Serious.'

Just then I heard the lock on my gas tank rattling, so I rushed outside with a shotgun and fired both barrels into the darkness. Poachers! I thought. Blow their heads off! This is War! So I fired another blast in the general direction of the gas pump, then I went inside to reload.

'Why are you shooting?' my assistant Anita screamed at me. 'What are you shooting at?'

'The enemy,' I said gruffly. 'He is down there stealing our gasoline.'

'Nonsense,' she said. 'That tank has been empty since June. You probably killed a peacock.'

At dawn I went down to the tank and found the gas hose shredded by birdshot and two peacocks dead.

So what? I thought. What is more important right now – my precious gasoline or the lives of some silly birds?

Indeed, but the New York Stock Exchange opened Monday morning, so I have to get a grip on something solid. The Other Shoe is about to drop, and it might be extremely heavy. The time has come to be strong. The fat is in the fire. Who knows what will happen now?

Not me, buster. That's why I live out here in the mountains with a flag on my porch and loud Wagner music blaring out of my speakers. I feel lucky, and I have plenty of ammunition. That is God's will, they say, and that is also why I shoot into the darkness at anything that moves. Sooner or later, I will hit something Evil and feel no Guilt. It might be Osama bin Laden. Who knows? And where is Adolf Hitler, now that we finally need him? It is bad business to go into War without a target.

In times like these, when the War drums roll and the bugles howl for blood, I think of Vince Lombardi, and I wonder how he would handle it . . . Good old Vince. He was a zealot for Victory at all costs, and his hunger for it was pure – or that's what he said and what his legend tells us, but it is worth noting that he is not even in the top 20 in career victories.

We are At War now, according to President Bush, and I take him at his word. He also says this War might last for 'a very long time'.

Generals and military scholars will tell you that 8 or

10 years is actually not such a long time in the span of human history – which is no doubt true – but history also tells us that 10 years of martial law and a wartime economy are going to feel like a Lifetime to people who are in their twenties today. The poor bastards of what will forever be known as Generation Z are doomed to be the first generation of Americans who will grow up with a lower standard of living than their parents enjoyed.

That is extremely heavy news, and it will take a while for it to sink in. The 22 babies born in New York City while the World Trade Center burned will never know what they missed. The last half of the 20th Century will seem like a wild party for rich kids, compared to what's coming now. The party's over, folks. The time has come for loyal Americans to Sacrifice . . . Sacrifice . . . Sacrifice. That is the new buzzword in Washington. But what it means is not entirely clear.

Winston Churchill said, 'The first casualty of War is always Truth.' Churchill also said, 'In wartime, Truth is so precious that she should always be attended by a bodyguard of Lies.'

That wisdom will not be much comfort to babies born last week. The first news they get in this world will be News subjected to Military Censorship. That is a given in wartime, along with massive campaigns of deliberately planted 'Dis-information'. That is routine behavior in Wartime – for all countries and all combatants – and it makes life difficult for people who value real news. Count on it. That is what Churchill meant when he talked about Truth being the first casualty of War.

In this case, however, the next casualty was Football. All games were canceled last week. And that has Never happened to the NFL. Never. That gives us a hint about the Magnitude of this War. Terrorists don't wear uniforms, and they play by inscrutable rules – The Rules of World War III, which has already begun.

So get ready for it, folks. Buckle up and watch your backs at all times. That is why they call it 'Terrorism'.

September 19, 2001

The Lion and the Cadillac

Fear? I know not fear. There are only moments of confusion. Some of them are deeply stamped on my memory and a few will haunt me forever.

One of my ugliest and most confused moments, I think, was when I was driving a junk Cadillac down the Coast Highway to Big Sur and a large mountain lion jumped into the moving car.

I had stopped for a moment beside the road to put out a newspaper fire in the backseat when this huge cat either jumped or fell off a cliff and landed on its back in the gravel right beside me. I was leaning over the side and pouring beer on the fire when it happened.

It was late in the day, and I was alone. When the beast hit the ground I had a moment of total confusion. And so did the lion. Then I jumped back in the car and took off down the hill in low gear, thinking to escape certain death or at least mutilation.

The beast had tried to pounce on me from above, but missed . . . And now, as I shifted the junker into second, I heard a terrible snarling and realized that the cat was running right behind me and gaining . . . (I was, in fact, Terrified at that moment.) . . . And I think I must have gone temporarily insane when the goddamn thing came up beside me and jumped right into the car through the passenger-side window like a bomb.

It bounced against the dashboard and somehow turned the radio volume all the way up. Then it clawed me badly on my arm and one leg. That is why I shudder every time I hear a Chuck Berry tune.

I can still smell the beast. I heard myself screaming as I tried to steer. There was blood all over the seat. The music was deafening and the cat was still snarling and clawing at me. Then it scrambled over the seat and into the back, right into the pile of still-burning newspapers. I heard a screech of pain and saw the cat trying to hurl itself through the back window.

We were still rolling along at about thirty miles per hour when I noticed my ball-peen hammer sticking out of the mangled glove compartment.

I grabbed the hammer with my right hand, steering with my left, and swung it wildly over my shoulder at the mountain lion.

Whack! I felt it hit something that felt vaguely like a carton of eggs, and then there was silence. No resistance in the backseat. Nothing.

I hit the brakes and pulled over. My hand was still on the hammer when I looked back and saw that I had somehow hit the animal squarely on top of its head and driven the iron ball right through its skull and into its brain. It was dead. Hunched on its back and filling the whole rear of the car, which was filling up with blood.

I was no longer confused.

Yesterday's Weirdness is Tomorrow's Reason Why

WILLIAM MCKEEN: *Your use of drugs is one of the more controversial things about you and your writing. Do you think the use of drugs has been exaggerated by the media? How have drugs affected your perception of the world and/or your writing? Does the media portrayal of you as a 'crazy' amuse, inflame, or bore you?*

HUNTER S. THOMPSON: Obviously, my drug use is exaggerated or I would be long since dead. I've already outlived the most brutal abuser of our time – Neal Cassady. Me and William Burroughs are the only other ones left. We're the last unrepentant public dope fiends, and he's seventy years old and claiming to be clean. But he hasn't turned on drugs, like that lying, treacherous, sold-out punk Timothy Leary.

Drugs usually enhance or strengthen my perceptions and reactions, for good or ill. They've given me the resilience to withstand repeated shocks to my innocence gland. The brutal reality of politics alone would probably be intolerable without drugs. They've given me the strength to deal with those shocking realities guaranteed to shatter *anyone's* beliefs in the higher idealistic shibboleths of our time and the 'American Century'. Anyone who covers his beat for twenty years – and my beat is 'The Death of the American Dream' – needs every goddamned crutch he can find.

Besides, I *enjoy* drugs. The only trouble they've given me is the people who try to keep me from using them. *Res Ipsa Loquitur*. I was, after all, a Literary Lion last year.

The media perception of me has always been pretty broad. As broad as the media itself. As a journalist, I somehow managed to break most of the rules and still succeed. It's a hard thing for most of today's journeyman journalists to understand, but only because they can't do it. The smart ones understood immediately. The best people in journalism I've never had any quarrel with. I *am* a journalist and I've never met, as a group, any tribe I'd rather be a part of or that are more fun to be with – despite the various punks and sycophants of the press.

It hasn't helped a lot to be a savage comic-book character for the last fifteen years – a drunken screwball who should've been castrated a long time ago. The smart people in the media knew it was a weird exaggeration. The dumb ones took it seriously and warned their children to stay away from me at all costs. The *really* smart ones understood it was only a censored, kind of toned-down, children's-book version of the real thing.

Now we are being herded into the nineties, which looks like it is going to be a *true* generation of swine, a decade run by cops with no humor, with dead heroes, and diminished expectations, a decade that will go down in history as The Gray Area. At the end of the decade, no one will be sure of anything except that you *must* obey the rules, sex will kill you, politicians lie, rain is poison, and the world is run by whores. These are terrible things to have to know in your life, even if you're rich.

Since it's become the mode, that sort of thinking has taken over the media, as it has business and politics: 'I'm going to turn you in, son – not just for your own good but because you were the bastard who turned *me* in last year.'

This vilification by Nazi elements within the media has not only given me a fierce joy to continue my work – more and more alone out here, as darkness falls on the barricades – but has also made me profoundly orgasmic, mysteriously rich, and constantly at war with those vengeful retro-fascist elements of the Establishment that have hounded me all my life. It has also made me wise, shrewd, and crazy on a level that can only be known by those who have been there.

WM: *Some libraries classify* **Fear and Loathing in Las Vegas** *as a travelogue, some classify it as non-fiction, and some classify it as a novel. How much of this book is true? How would you characterize this book (beyond the jacket copy info in* **The Great Shark Hunt***)? You refer to it as a failed experiment in Gonzo journalism, yet many critics consider it a masterwork. How would you rate it?*

HST: *Fear and Loathing in Las Vegas* is a masterwork. However, true Gonzo journalism as I conceive it shouldn't be rewritten.

I would classify it, in Truman Capote's words, as a non-fiction novel in that almost all of it was true or *did* happen. I warped a few things, but it was a pretty accurate picture. It was an incredible feat of balance more than literature. That's why I called it *Fear and Loathing*. It was a pretty pure experience that turned into a very pure piece of writing. It's as good as *The Great Gatsby* and better than *The Sun Also Rises*.

WM: *For years your readers have heard about* **The Rum Diary**. *Are you working on it, or on any other novel? Do you have an ambition to write fiction? Your stint as a newspaper columnist was successful, but do you have further ambitions within journalism?*

HST: I've always had and still do have an ambition to write fiction. I've never had any real ambition within journalism, but events and fate and my own sense of fun keep taking me back for money, political reasons, and because I am a warrior. I haven't found a drug yet that can get you anywhere near as high as sitting at a desk writing, trying to imagine a story no matter how bizarre it is, as much as going out and getting into the weirdness of reality and doing a little time on The Proud Highway.

March 1990

May You Live in Interesting Times

There is an ancient Chinese curse that says, 'May you live in interesting times', which was told to me by an elderly dope fiend on a rainy night in Hong Kong near the end of the War in Vietnam. He was a giddy old man, on the surface, but I knew – and he knew that I knew – of the fear and respect he commanded all over Southeast Asia as a legendary Wizard in the far-flung Kingdom of Opium. I had stopped by his shop in Kowloon to get some advice and a chunk of black medicine for my friends who were trapped in the NVA noose that was inexorably closing in on Saigon. They refused to leave, they said, but in order to stay alive in the doomed and dysfunctional city, they needed only two things – cash money and fine opium.

I was no stranger to either one of these things, at the time – and I was, after all, in Hong Kong. All I had to do to get a satchel of green money and pure opium delivered to the *Newsweek* bureau was make a few phone calls. My friends trapped in Saigon were Journalists. We have a strong sense, people of my own breed and tribe, and we are linked – especially in war zones – by strong bonds of tribal loyalty . . .

One Hand Clapping

I knew a Buddhist once, and I've hated myself ever since. The whole thing was a failure.

He was a priest of some kind, and he was also extremely rich. They called him a monk and he wore the saffron robes and I hated him because of his arrogance. He thought he knew everything.

One day I was trying to rent a large downtown property from him, and he mocked me. 'You are dumb,' he said. 'You are doomed if you stay in this business. The stupid are gobbled up quickly.'

'I understand,' I said. 'I am stupid. I am doomed. But I think I know something you don't.'

He laughed. 'Nonsense,' he said. 'You are a fool. You know nothing.'

I nodded respectfully and leaned closer to him, as if to whisper a secret. 'I know the answer to the greatest riddle of all,' I said.

He chuckled. 'And what is that?' he said. 'And you'd better be Right, or I'll kill you.'

'I know the sound of one hand clapping,' I said. 'I have finally discovered the answer.'

Several other Buddhists in the room laughed out loud, at this point. I knew they wanted to humiliate me, and now they had me trapped – because there *is* no answer to that question. These saffron bastards have been teasing us with it forever. They are amused at our failure to grasp it.

Ho ho. I went into a drastic crouch and hung my left hand low, behind my knee. 'Lean closer,' I said to him. 'I want to answer your high and unanswerable question.'

As he leaned his bright bald head a little closer into my orbit, I suddenly leaped up and bashed him flat on the ear with the palm of my left hand. It was slightly cupped, so as to deliver maximum energy on impact. An isolated package of air is suddenly driven through the Eustachian tube and into the middle brain at quantum speed, causing pain, fear, and extreme insult to the tissue.

The monk staggered sideways and screamed, grasping his head in agony. Then he fell to the floor and cursed me. 'You swine!' he croaked. 'Why did you hit me and burst my eardrum?'

'Because *that*,' I said, 'is the sound of one hand clapping. That is the answer to your question. I have the answer now, and you are deaf.'

'Indeed,' he said. 'I am deaf, but I am smarter. I am wise in a different way.' He grinned vacantly and reached out to shake my hand.

'You're welcome,' I said. 'I am, after all, a doctor.'

It Never Got Weird Enough for Me

Dear Dr. Thompson,

My name is Xania and I am very beautiful and my family is very rich. I am eight years old and I live in Turkey. We live by the sea, but I am bored here. They treat me like a child, but I am not. I am ready to escape. I want to leave. I want to get married and I want to marry *you*. That is why I write you today. I want you to suck my tits while I scream and dance in your lap and my mother watches. She is the one who says this. She loves you very much and so do I.

I am eight years old and my body is well advanced. My mother is twenty-six and, boy! You should see *her*. We are almost twins and so is my grandmother, who is only forty-two years old and looks the same as me. I think she is crazy like my mother. They are beautiful when they walk around naked, and so am I. We are always naked here. We are rich and the sea is so beautiful. If the sea had brains, I would suck them out of it. But I can't. The sea has no penis.

Why is that, Doc? If you are so smart, answer *that* one! Fuck you. I knew you wouldn't help us. Please send three plane tickets right *now*. I love you! We are *not* whores. Please help me. I know I will see you soon. We travel a lot. My father wants you to marry me. He is sixty-six years old and he owns the main banks of Turkey. All of them. We will have a beautiful, beautiful wedding when you show them us naked and I dance while you suck my tits and my father screams. O God I love you! Our dream is now. Yes.

Your baby,
Xania

Heeere's Johnny!

FEAR AND LOATHING AT JACK'S HOUSE . . .
THE LONELIEST PLACE IN THE WORLD

It was a dark and stormy night when I set out from my house to Jack Nicholson's place far away in a valley on the other side of town. It was his birthday, and I had a huge raw elk heart for him. I have known Jack for many years, and we share a certain sense of humor among other things, and in truth there was nothing inherently strange in the notion of bringing a freshly taken elk heart out to his home on the night of his birthday.

It was lightly frozen and beginning to leak from the chambers, so I put it in a Ziploc bag and tossed it in the back of the Jeep. Hot damn, I thought, Jack's children will love this. I knew they had just arrived that day from Los Angeles, and I wanted to have a surprise for them. 'You won't be late, will you?' Jack had asked. 'You know the kids go to bed early.'

'Don't worry,' I said. 'I'm leaving in ten minutes.'

And it was just about then that the night began to go wrong. Time withered away. Some kind of episode occurred, and before I knew it I was running two hours late – two hours, keep that in mind because it will make a difference later on.

Okay. So I set out to see Jack and his children with all kinds of jokes and gimcracks in my car. In addition to the bleeding elk heart, there was a massive outdoor amplifier, a tape recording of a pig being eaten alive by bears, a 1,000,000-watt spotlight, and a 9-mm Smith & Wesson semiautomatic pistol with teakwood handles and a box of high-powered ammunition. There was also a 40-million-candlepower parachute flare that would light up the valley for 40 miles for 40 seconds that would seem to anyone lucky enough to be awake at the time like the first blinding flash of a midrange nuclear device that might signal the end of the world. It was a hand-held mortar, in fact, with a plastic lanyard on one end and the black snout of a firing tube on the other. I had found it on sale a few weeks earlier at West Marine Hardware in Sausalito for $115, down from $210. It was irresistible – even cheap, I felt, for such a spectacular display – and I was looking forward to using it. The directions were vague, and mainly in foreign languages, but the diagrams made it clear that The USER should wear suitable eye protection, hold projectile vertically as far from body as possible, then JERK FIRING RING STRAIGHT DOWN and DO NOT ALLOW PROJECT-ILE TO TILT.

Okay, I thought, I can do this. I know flares. I have fired those huge gray military things, where you pull off one end and put it on the other, then bash your palm against the bottom and feel both your arms go numb all the way up to your skull from an explosion equal to a 105-mm howitzer blast. So I wasn't worried about this cheap red load from Sausalito. Once you get a feeling for handling nitroglycerine fuses, you never lose it.

I was thinking about these things as I wound my way up the long winding road to Jack's house. It was ten miles of darkness, and by the time I got there I was feeling a little jumpy, so I pulled over and parked on a bluff overlooking the Nicholson home.

There were no other cars on the road. I unloaded the huge amplifier and mounted it firmly on top of the Jeep. The horn pointed out across the valley, then I placed the flare neatly beside it and leaned back against the hood to smoke a cigarette. Far down through the pines I could see the queer-looking lights of Jack's house. The night was extremely quiet and the LED in my Jeep said it was nine degrees above zero and the time was no later than 2:30 A.M., or maybe 2:45. I remember hearing a gospel tune on the radio, then I plugged the horn into the amplifier and beamed up the pig-screaming tape to about 119 decibels.

The noise was intolerable, at first. I had to cover my head and crouch behind the Jeep to get away from it. I wanted to turn it off, but just then I saw headlights coming up the road and I had to get out of sight . . . The car never even slowed down as it passed me, despite the hideous screams of what sounded like a whole herd of pigs being slaughtered.

My first thought, for some reason, was that it was not Bill Clinton, because he would have at least honked. Ho ho, good joke, eh? It's odd how Bill Clinton jokes seem to pop up at unnatural moments like these – when you're doing something that feels deeply right and normal and you feel in a high sense of humor as you set about your task, which then somehow goes wrong for reasons beyond your control and sows the seeds of tragedy.

Nobody needs this – but some people seem to want it, and on that giddy winter night in the Rockies, I was one of them. No power of reason or nature could have persuaded me that the small, friendly, and finely organized chain of events already in motion would not be received by the family down below with anything but joy, surprise, and gratitude.

I kept the amplifier going with the pig screams every twenty or thirty seconds, bracketed around bursts of rapid gunfire – and then I put the million-watt strobe down on the house, dragging it back and forth across the deck and the living room windows.

I did this for ten minutes or so, but nothing happened. The only response from below was a silent spasm of lights being turned off, as if they were all going to bed.

Well, I thought, that is a rude way to act when guests come with presents, even if they are a bit late. So what? There is no excuse for rudeness.

My next move was potentially fatal. I attempted to launch the rocket, but the firing ring broke and the thing started hissing, so I quickly hurled it away and heard it tumbling down the hill toward the house. O God, I thought, those are magnum phosphorous flares, and this place is going to be like the bridge in *Apocalypse Now* when that goddamn thing explodes.

I hastily packed the amp into the Jeep and picked up as many of my empty brass cartridges as I could find in the snow – and it was then, as I fled, that I remembered my birthday gift, which had somehow popped out of its bag and was bleeding all over the backseat.

I was beginning to have mixed feelings about this visit. There was something out of whack, and I figured the best thing to do was get out of this valley immediately. There was only one road out. (If some worrywart had called 911 to report an outburst of screaming and shooting at the Nicholson place, that could pose a problem, given that I was far down at the end of a dead-end canyon with no other way to escape but the river, and that was not an option.)

But *why?* I thought. Why am I drifting into negativity? Never mind this talk about 'escape'. I am here on a mission of joy. And there are no neighbors, anyway. It was a dark and peaceful place – yet extremely desolate in many ways, and not a good place to be trapped in.

I dismissed these negative thoughts as I hooked a hard left into Jack's driveway, intent on delivering my birthday present. The iron jackals on the gateposts no longer disturbed me, and I knew I could do this thing quickly.

I drove the Jeep all the way up to the front door and left the motor running as I fetched the bleeding elk heart out of the backseat and carried it up to the house. I rang the doorbell a few times before I gave up and left the heart – about ten inches tall and seven inches wide

– propped against the door in a way that would cause it to tumble into the house whenever the door was opened. It seemed like the right thing to do, in light of the rudeness I'd experienced, and panic was setting in. On my way back to the truck I made sure the gun was clear by cranking off the rest of the clip straight up in the air and flinging my bloody hands distractedly toward the house because I was sure I'd seen somebody watching me from inside the darkened kitchen window, which angered me even further, because I felt I was being snubbed.

But I left quickly, with no other noise or weirdness except the shooting, which sounded unnaturally loud and caused pain in both of my eardrums. I jerked the Jeep into low and whiplashed out to the road. It was time to go home and sleep heavily – and there were no signs of police or any other disturbance as I drove carefully down the icy road. I locked in on Venus, the Morning Star, and pulled safely into my garage before sunrise.

The rest of the morning was spent in a work frenzy. My fax machine beeped constantly. There were the usual messages from the White House, two dangerously bogus offers from Hollywood, and a 60-page, single-spaced transcript of General Douglas MacArthur's final address to The Long Gray Line of steely-eyed cadets on The Plain at West Point in the spring of 1962, and another 39 pages of his 'Old Soldiers Never Die' speech to Congress after he'd been fired.

These things spew into my house day after day, and

I do my best to analyze them. Different people want different things in this world, and you have to be careful about taking risks. Hungry people have the cunning of wild beasts. A thing that seemed strange and wrong yesterday can seem perfectly reasonable tomorrow, or vice versa.

It did not seem strange, for instance, to learn that Bill Clinton's main concern these days is with his place in history, his legacy, his permanent image in high-school textbooks 100 years from now. He has done his work, he feels, and now is the time to secure his place on a pedestal in the pantheon of Great American Presidents, along with Lincoln and Coolidge and Kennedy.

And why not? George Bush had that problem, and so did Richard Nixon. Nobody needs to go down in history like that. Only a criminal freak would want to be remembered as a Crook or a Dupe or a Creature of some treacherous monster like J. Edgar Hoover . . . But those risks come with the territory when you finally move into the White House. You bet. They *will* write something – many things, in fact: books, movies, legends, and maybe even filthy jokes about back-stabbing and sodomy that will follow you all the way to the grave. Look at Nixon, look at Reagan, or even JFK. History has never been gentle in its judgments on bedrock degenerates – but it is also true that some degenerates are treated more gently than others, and that is what worries Bill Clinton. He is liked, but not well liked, and that is a very fragile base to maintain for another two and a half years. Voters *like* him now because they believe he has made them richer – and they will probably vote for Al Gore in 2000. (Jesus. That has an eerie ring to it, eh? *Vote Gore in 2000*. Prepare yourself for that. It will happen. Beware.)

I was brooding on these things on that bright winter morning when the phone machine rang and I heard a female voice screeching hysterically: 'Watch out, the police are coming' and 'Blood Everywhere' and 'Terrible tragedy at Jack's house last night.'

Ye gods, I thought. What is she talking about? What tragedy? Hell, I was there at about three and the place looked peaceful to me. What could have happened?

The answer was not long in coming. Both phones rang at once, but I suddenly felt queasy and couldn't answer. Then I heard the voice of the sheriff on one phone and some angry raving on the other from Paul Pascarella, the famous artist, who said he was on his way to Jack's house at top speed with a shotgun and a .44 Magnum. The house was under siege, he said. Cops were everywhere. Some maniac stalker tried to kill Jack and the kids last night, but he got away and the cops think he's still loose in the woods. He's a killer, just got out of prison, I think Jack's okay, O God this is horrible. Then he went into the canyon and lost contact.

The sheriff's message told much the same tale. 'This is going to be a very big story,' he said. 'I'm already setting up a command post to deal with the national media. They're calling it an assassination attempt. We've closed off the road and sent a posse with dogs to search the area. It's a manhunt. We'll be on CNN by noon –

and, by the way, do you happen to know anything about this? If you do, please call me before it's too late.'

Too late? I thought. Nonsense. Too late for what? Are we dealing with lunatics here? Why would I want to kill Jack? It was madness.

Indeed, and it was just about then that it hit me. Of course. That's me that they're chasing with dogs out there in the woods. *I* am the crazed bushy-haired assassin who tried to get into the house last night and murder the whole family. What the hell? It was only a joke.

A joke? Ho ho. Nobody else was laughing. They had already found an unexploded rocket bomb in the trees above the house . . . Every cop in the county was cranked up and working double-overtime to capture this monster before he could butcher the whole Nicholson family and bring eternal shame on Aspen's already sleazy name. Hideous scandals involving rich perverts, depraved children, and degenerate Hollywood whores looking for publicity are so common here as to be polit-ically tolerable and even stylish . . . Indeed, *that* is why this shit-rain of 'second-home pimps' has invaded this valley like a plague of rich lice in recent years . . . And we are not talking about small-time lice here, not at all.

Ah, but I digress. We were talking about my failed attempt to deliver some birthday presents to my old friend Jack and his kids on a frozen snowy night in the winter of 1997.

The *real* problem on that night turned out to be some-thing that did not occur to me, at the time – if only because it was so queer and unlikely as to beam new light on words like *incredible, bizarre*, and *impossible* . . .

But it happened, for good or ill – and now that I mention it, 4,000–1 tragedies like this one are the main reason I decided to renounce conventional crime as a way of life so many, many years ago – and turn to the writing life.

Jack had been menaced in public by a murderous certified *stalker* who had made several previous attempts on his life in Los Angeles – and the reason he had come to the Rockies was to be completely anonymous and solitary with Raymond and Lorraine, safe from the perils of Hollywood. He was, in a word, on the *lam* – just another jittery parent whose children had arrived to join him at his utterly isolated cabin home in the Rockies.

Who could have known, for instance, that *all* telephone service to Jack's bleak valley would be cut off by the blizzard that night? . . . 'Yeah, it was right about then that the phones went dead,' the sheriff told me. 'They tried to call 911, but the phone lines had apparently been cut. That's when he flipped out and barricaded the family in the basement behind a heap of antique furniture with nothing at all for a weapon except a common fireplace poker.' He chuckled. 'The fool didn't even have a gun in the house. Thank God for that, eh? He could have killed the children by accident.'

Which was true. As a *rule* it is better *not* to keep loaded weapons lying around the house when children are visiting. Even with a criminally insane stalker creeping around outside with a chainsaw. It is a far far better thing to have good locks and screechers on the doors, and a fulltime phone to the police station . . . This turned out to be no comfort at all to Jack and his family that night. The freak outside had a grudge, and he had come a long way to settle it. The setting was made to order (just like in *The Shining*).

The phones kept ringing and the news kept getting worse. Some people begged me to confess and others urged me to hurry out to Jack's with a 12-gauge riot gun and join the search party. Everybody who called seemed genuinely alarmed and afraid. Even Heidi was acting weird. She knew I had gone out to Jack's the previous night, and for all I knew she thought I'd tried to kill him for some reason. Why not? I might have had a seizure and flipped out. Who knows what a dope fiend might do? Especially with children around. I might not even remember it.

The phone rang again, and this time it was Jack. He had just got the phone working again. *Oh God*, I thought. *What am I going to say? Get a grip on yourself. Omerta.*

'Uh, Doc, how you doing?' he said calmly. It may have been a Saturday, because he said something like 'Who's playing this afternoon?'

'Never mind those fucking football games,' I said. 'What's this nightmare about the police out there at your house? I'm hearing weird things about it.'

There was a silence, a pause. I could hear him taking a breath. He said, 'Well, yeah, let me ask you a thing or two.' He paused. 'You know, that elk heart . . .'

That's what really freaked him out, all that blood. He said, 'When I looked at it – we were looking at it for clues' – I guessed he was talking about the cops – 'when

I took a close look at it, I saw that there were icicles in the middle of the heart, the part that still hadn't thawed. I didn't say anything to the cops, of course, but it seems like I remember you keeping a frozen elk heart in your refrigerator. Didn't you show me something like that, along with a bird and a ferret? Don't I remember you throwing a frozen elk heart at me last winter?'

That fucker, I thought. *The creepy little bastard*. That was good, putting that together – just a *sliver* inside, frozen. All the rest had turned to mush and blood – it's actually pretty good to eat, elk heart . . . this one wasn't going to be eaten anytime soon; it looked like a gizzard of some human being. Bigger than a human heart. 'Yeah, maybe . . .' I said.

'I thought so, I thought it was you, when I saw that ice,' he said. 'I haven't told them yet; you know, they're still out here, the police task force, digging for new evidence, people sleeping in the woods . . . Goddamn, Doc, I'm glad you told me. We have had a hell of a night here. It's been horrible.'

The joke was over. I was never formally accused of it; Jack told the sheriff it was just a false alarm. 'I know this guy,' he said, 'and he is not the killer.'

Epilogue

That is what I mean about personal security in this town. You can buy a lot of protection, if you are filthy rich, and it obviously makes those people feel better about themselves – surrounded at all times by hundreds of greedy freelance cops with a license to kill anytime, anywhere, for any reason blessed by God. They are volatile people, at best, and always dangerous.

We get more black-truck security caravans in this valley than anyplace in the world that comes quickly to mind except Washington, DC, and Vatican City. There is a lot of available cash in these places, a lot of quasi-secret money changing hands . . . of governments being toppled on the other side of the world, of kingdoms being undermined, and whole families of US presidents and movie stars like Julia Roberts and Harry Dean Stanton being bought and sold and coddled like concubines, by criminal scum like Neil Bush, convicted crook and brother of our sitting president George W. . . . Not to mention the current Secretary of the (US) Army and gilded clutch of criminally fugitive executives from ENRON, including the monstrous chairman Kenneth Lay . . . These people roam free and unmolested in Aspen, cloistered by off-duty cops and Hollywood yo-yos and bimbos and suckfish . . . I know these people. They are more and more my neighbors in these first horrible years of our new Century . . .

There is never any shortage of applicants for *paid*-police jobs in the Roaring Fork Valley. All ambitious young cops want to be hired in places like Palm Beach and Sausalito and Aspen. They crave their 15 minutes of fame, and their police research has told them that Aspen is the most likely place to get it . . .

Which is normal enough in this town. It has long been a haven for sybaritic outlaws and other social criminals as long as they had a good story and didn't hurt the neighbors – not quite a *sanctuary*, but at least a sort of retro-legal gray area, where real-life words like Crime and Guilt mean different things to different people, even in the same household.

Fear and Loathing at the Taco Stand

Going to Hollywood is a dangerous high-pressure gig for most people, under any circumstances. It is like pumping hot steam into thousands of different-size boilers. The laws of physics mandate that some will explode before others – although all of them will explode sooner or later unless somebody cuts off the steam.

I love steam myself, and I have learned to survive under savage and unnatural pressures. I am a steam freak. Hollywood is chicken feed to me. I can take it or leave it. I have been here before, many times. On some days it seems like I have lived at the Château Marmont for half my life. There is blood on these walls, and some of it is mine. Last night I sliced off the tips of two fingers and bled so profusely in the elevator that they had to take it out of service.

But nobody complained. I am not just liked at the Château, I am well liked. I have important people thrown out or blacklisted on a whim. Nobody from the Schwarzenegger organization, for instance, can even get a drink at the Château. They are verboten. There is a ghastly political factor in doing any business with Hollywood. You can't get by without five or six personal staff people – and at least one personal astrologer.

I have always hated astrologers, and I like to have

sport with them. They are harmless quacks in the main, but some of them get ambitious and turn predatory, especially in Hollywood. In Venice Beach I ran into a man who claimed to be Johnny Depp's astrologer. 'I consult with him constantly,' he told me. 'We are never far away. I have many famous clients.' He produced a yellow business card and gave it to me. 'I can do things for you,' he said. 'I am a player.'

I took his card and examined it carefully for a moment, as if I couldn't quite read the small print. But I knew he was lying, so I leaned toward him and slapped him sharply in the nuts. Not hard, but very quickly, using the back of my hand and my fingers like a bull-whip, yet very discreetly.

He let out a hiss and went limp, unable to speak or breathe. I smiled casually and kept on talking to him as if nothing had happened. 'You filthy little creep,' I said to him. 'I *am* Johnny Depp!'

Outside on the boulevard I saw a half-naked girl on roller skates being mauled by two dogs. They were Great Danes, apparently running loose. Both had their paws on her shoulder, and the gray one had her head in its mouth. But there was no noise, and nobody seemed to notice.

I grabbed a fork off the bar and rushed outside to help her, giving the bogus astrologer another slap in the nuts on my way out. When I got to the street, the dogs were still mauling the girl. I stabbed the big one in the ribs with my fork, which sank deep into the tissue. The beast yelped crazily and ran off with its tail between its legs. The other one quickly released its grip on the girl's head and snarled at me. I slashed at it with the fork, and that was enough for the brute. It backed off and slunk away toward Muscle Beach.

I took the girl back to the Buffalo Club and applied aloe to her wounds. The astrologer was gone, and we had the lounge to ourselves. Her name was Anita, she said, and she had just arrived in LA to seek work as a dancer. It was the third time in ten days she'd been attacked by wild dogs on the Venice boardwalk, and she was ready to quit LA, and so was I. The pace was getting to me. I was not bored, and I still had work to do, but it was definitely time to get out of town. I had to be in Big Sur in three days, and then to a medical conference in Pebble Beach. She was a very pretty girl, with elegant legs and a wicked kind of intelligence about her, but she was also very naïve about Hollywood. I saw at once that she would be extremely helpful on my trip north.

I listened to her for a while, then I offered her a job as my assistant, which I badly needed. She accepted, and we drove back to the Château in Depp's Porsche. As we pulled up the ramp to the underground garage, the attendants backed off and signaled me in. Depp's henchmen had left word that nobody could touch the car except me. I parked it expertly, barely missing a red BMW 840Ci, and we went up the elevator to my suite.

I reached for my checkbook, but it was missing, so I used one of Depp's that I'd found in the glove compartment of his car. I wrote her a healthy advance and signed Depp's name to it. 'What the hell?' I said to her. 'He's running around out there with my checkbook right now, probably racking up all kinds of bills.'

That was the tone of my workdays in Hollywood: violence, joy, and constant Mexican music. At one club I played the bass recorder for several hours with the band. We spent a lot of time drinking gin and lemonade on the balcony, entertaining movie people and the ever-present scribe from *Rolling Stone* magazine . . .

You bet, Bubba, I was taking care of business. It was like the Too Much Fun Club. I had the Cadillac and a green Mustang in the garage, in addition to the Carrera 4 Porsche, but we could only drive one of them up the coast. It was an uptown problem.

Finally it got to be too much, so we loaded up the Northstar Cadillac and fled. Why not? I thought. The girl had proved to be a tremendous help, and besides, I was beginning to like her.

The sun was going down as we left Malibu and headed north on 101, running smoothly through Oxnard and along the ocean to Santa Barbara. My companion was a little nervous about my speed, so I gave her some gin to calm her down. Soon she relaxed against me, and I put my arm around her. Rosanne Cash was on the radio, singing about the seven-year ache, and the traffic was opening up.

As we approached the Lompoc exit, I mentioned that Lompoc was the site of a federal penitentiary and I once had some friends over there.

'Oh?' she said. 'Who were they?'

'Prisoners,' I said. 'Nothing serious. That's where Ed was.'

She stiffened and moved away from me, but I turned up the music and we settled back to drive and watch the moon come up. What the hell? I thought. Just another young couple on the road to the American Dream.

Things started to get weird when I noticed Pismo Beach coming up. I was on the cell phone with Benicio Del Toro, the famous Puerto Rican actor, telling him about the time I was violently jailed in Pismo Beach and how it was making me nervous to even pass a road sign with that name on it. 'Yeah,' I was saying, 'it was horrible. They beat me on the back of my legs. It was a case of mistaken identity.' I smiled at my assistant, not wanting to alarm her, but I saw that she was going into a fetal crouch and her fingers were clutching the straps of her seat belt.

Just then we passed two police cars parked on the side of the road, and I saw that we were going a hundred and three.

'Slow down!' Anita was screaming. 'Slow down! We'll be arrested. I can't stand it!' She was sobbing and clawing at the air.

'Nonsense,' I said. 'Those were not police. My radar didn't go off.' I reached over to pat her on the arm, but she bit me and I had to pull over. The only exit led to a dangerous-looking section of Pismo Beach, but I took it anyway.

It was just about midnight when we parked under the streetlight in front of the empty Mexican place on Main

Street. Anita was having a nervous breakdown. There was too much talk about jails and police and prisons, she said. She felt like she was already in chains.

I left the car in a crosswalk and hurried inside to get a taco. The girl behind the register warned me to get my car off the street because the police were about to swoop down on the gang of thugs milling around in front of the taco place. 'They just had a fight with the cops,' she said. 'Now I'm afraid somebody is going to get killed.'

We were parked right behind the doomed mob, so I hurried out to roust Anita and move the car to safety. Then we went back inside very gently and sat down in a booth at the rear of the room. I put my arm around Anita and tried to calm her down. She wanted gin, and luckily I still had a pint flask full of it in my fleece-lined jacket pocket. She drank greedily, then fell back in the booth and grinned. 'Well, so much for that,' she chirped. 'I guess I really went crazy, didn't I?'

'Yes,' I said. 'You were out of control. It was like dealing with a vampire.'

She smiled and grasped my thigh. 'I am a vampire,' she said. 'We have many a mile to go before we sleep. I am hungry.'

'Indeed,' I said. 'We will have to fill up on tacos before we go any farther. I too am extremely hungry.'

Just then the waitress arrived to take our order. The mob of young Chicanos outside had disappeared very suddenly, roaring off into the night in a brace of white pickup trucks. They were a good-natured bunch, mainly teenagers with huge shoulders wearing Dallas Cowboys jerseys and heads like half-shaved coconuts. They were not afraid of the cops, but they left anyway.

The waitress was hugely relieved. 'Thank God,' she said. 'Now Manuel can live one more night. I was afraid they would kill him. We have only been married three weeks.' She began sobbing, and I could see she was about to crack. I introduced myself as Johnny Depp, but I saw the name meant nothing to her. Her name was Maria. She was seventeen years old and had lied about her age to get the job. She was the manager and Manuel was the cook. He was almost twenty-one. Every night strange men hovered around the taco stand and mumbled about killing him.

Maria sat down in the booth between us, and we both put our arms around her. She shuddered and collapsed against Anita, kissing her gently on the cheek. 'Don't worry,' I said. 'Nobody is going to be killed tonight. This is the night of the full moon. Some people will die tonight, but not us. I am protected.'

Which was true. I am a Triple Moon Child, and tonight was the Hunter's Moon. I pulled the waitress closer to me and spoke soothingly. 'You have nothing to fear, little one,' I told her. 'No power on Earth can harm me tonight. I walk with the King.'

She smiled and kissed me gratefully on the wrist. Manuel stared balefully at us from his perch in the kitchen, saying nothing. 'Rest easy,' I called out to him. 'Nobody is going to kill you tonight.'

'Stop saying that!' Anita snapped, as Manuel sank further into himself. 'Can't you see he's afraid?' Maria began crying again, but I jerked her to her feet. 'Get a grip on yourself,' I said sharply. 'We need more beer and some pork tacos to go. I have to drive the whole coast tonight.'

'That's right,' said my companion. 'We're on a honeymoon trip. We're in a hurry.' She laughed and reached for my wallet. 'Come on, big boy,' she cooed. 'Don't try to cheat. Just give it to me.'

'Watch yourself,' I snarled, slapping her hand away from my pocket. 'You've been acting weird ever since we left LA. We'll be in serious trouble if you go sideways on me again.'

She grinned and stretched her arms lazily above her head, poking her elegant little breasts up in the air at me like some memory from an old Marilyn Monroe calendar and rolling her palms in the air.

'Sideways?' she said. 'What difference does it make? Let's get out of here. We're late.'

I paid the bill quickly and watched Maria disappear into the kitchen. Manuel was nowhere in sight. Just as I stepped into the street, I noticed two police cars coming at us from different directions. Then another one slowed down right in front of the taco stand.

'Don't worry,' I said to Anita. 'They're not looking for us.'

I seized her by the leg and rushed her into the Cadillac. There was a lot of yelling as we pulled away through the circling traffic and back out onto Highway 101.

My mind was very much on my work as we sped north along the coast to Big Sur. We were into open country now, running straight up the coast about a mile from the ocean on a two-lane blacktop road across the dunes with no clouds in the sky and a full moon blazing down on the Pacific. It was a perfect night to be driving a fast car on an empty road along the edge of the ocean with a half-mad beautiful woman asleep on the white leather seats and Lyle Lovett crooning doggerel about screwheads who go out to sea with shotguns and ponies in small rowboats just to get some kind of warped revenge on a white man with bad habits who was only trying to do them a favor in the first place.

I lost control of the Cadillac about halfway down the slope. The road was slick with pine needles, and the eucalyptus trees were getting closer together. The girl laughed as I tried to aim the car through the darkness with huge tree trunks looming up in the headlights and the bright white moon on the ocean out in front of us. It was like driving on ice, going straight toward the abyss.

We shot past a darkened house and past a parked Jeep, then crashed into a waterfall high above the sea. I got out of the car and sat down on a rock, then lit up the marijuana pipe. 'Well,' I said to Anita, 'this is it. We must have taken a wrong turn.'

She laughed and sucked on some moss. Then she sat down across from me on a log. 'You're funny,' she said. 'You're very strange – and you don't know why, do you?'

I shook my head softly and drank some gin.

'No,' I said. 'I'm stupid.'

'It's because you have the soul of a teenage girl in

the body of an elderly dope fiend,' she whispered. 'That is why you have problems.' She patted me on the knee. 'Yes. That is why people giggle with fear every time you come into a room. That is why you rescued me from those dogs in Venice.'

I stared out to sea and said nothing for a while. But somehow I knew she was right. Yes sir, I said slowly to myself, I have the soul of a teenage girl in the body of an elderly dope fiend. No wonder they can't understand me.

This is a hard dollar, on most days, and not many people can stand it.

Indeed. If the greatest mania of all is passion: and if I am a natural slave to passion: and if the balance between my brain and my soul and my body is as wild and delicate as the skin of a Ming vase –

Well, that explains a lot of things, doesn't it? We need look no further. Yes sir, and people wonder why I seem to look at them strangely. Or why my personal etiquette often seems makeshift and contradictory, even clinically insane . . . Hell, I don't miss those whispers, those soft groans of fear when I enter a civilized room. I know what they're thinking, and I know exactly why. They are extremely uncomfortable with the idea that I am a teenage girl trapped in the body of a sixty-five-year-old career criminal who has already died sixteen times. Sixteen, all documented. I have been crushed and beaten and shocked and drowned and poisoned and stabbed and shot and smothered and set on fire by my own bombs . . .

All these things have happened, and probably they

will happen again. I have learned a few tricks along the way, a few random skills and simple avoidance techniques – but mainly it has been luck, I think, and a keen attention to karma, along with my natural girlish charm.

POCKET PENGUINS

POCKET PENGUINS